IRISH MARRIAGE CUSTOMS

First published in 2000 by
Mercier Press
PO Box 5 5 French Church St Cork
Tel: (021) 275040; Fax: (021) 274969; e.mail: books@mercier.ie
16 Hume Street Dublin 2
Tel: (01) 661 5299; Fax: (01) 661 8583; e.mail: books@marino.ie

Trade enquiries to CMD Distribution 55A Spruce Avenue
Stillorgan Industrial Park Blackrock County Dublin
Tel: (01) 294 2556; Fax: (01) 294 2564
e.mail: cmd@columba.ie

ISBN 1 85635 306 0
10 9 8 7 6 5 4 3 2 1

Cover photograph courtesy The Ulster Folk and Transport Museum
Cultra County Down
Cover design by Penhouse Design
Printed by Cox and Wyman Reading Berkshire UK

IRISH MARRIAGE CUSTOMS

MARIA BUCKLEY

MERCIER PRESS

In memory of my parents,
who married for love

ACKNOWLEDGEMENTS

I would like to acknowledge the debt this short account of marriage customs in Ireland owes to three writers in particular: Kevin Danaher (*In Ireland Long Ago, The Year in Ireland*); Éamon Kelly (*The Apprentice, Ireland's Master Storyteller*) and Linda May Ballard (*Forgetting Frolic: Marriage Traditions in Ireland*). Specific references to these works are made in the text and bibliography. Although Éamon Kelly is a seanchaí, not a folklorist, his stories are excellent sources for the customs of the first half of the twentieth century. I offer thanks to Mercier Press, the publishers of the works of Éamon Kelly and Kevin Danaher, for permission to quote from these authors' books.

CONTENTS

Contents

1

I KNOW MY LOVE
MARRIAGE DIVINATION

I know where I'm going
And I know who'll go with me
I know who I love
But the dear knows who I'll marry

go the words of the old song. Marriage was a
matter of great importance in traditional Irish
society, for women – in the absence of any career
opportunities or financial independence – and
for men in rural society because of the necessity
of producing an heir to succeed to the family
farm, no matter how humble a holding it might
be. Affairs of the heart were then, as always, a
matter of some perplexity and frequent heart-
break. Is there a woman alive, no matter how
modern, who has not at some stage of her early

life plucked the petals off a daisy while chanting 'He loves me/He loves me not.' Divination, the art of finding out the name or appearance of your true love or the man you were going to marry, was very commonly practised in Irish society of yesteryear, especially among young or marriageable women. It reached far greater complexity (some might say absurdity) than that simple, homely ritual with the daisy. Yet many of the strategies and ceremonies are still familiar to us today.

Hallowe'en was the festival most strongly associated with divination. An agricultural people had more leisure during the winter to plan the romances and matches for the weddings that were to take place the following Shrove. The dark evenings and the aura of the supernatural around the pagan festival of Samhain, which dated from very ancient days in Ireland, were conducive to thoughts of courtship and romance.

The first category of divination practised at Hallowe'en related to the fate of the individual. One of the possible fates was marriage, so this kind of divination was meant to indicate whether the woman or man would marry at all.

The best known of the Hallowe'en customs, and the one that is most popular today, relates to the barmbrack. The objects mixed in the dough and baked in the cake to be found by a member of the family or one of the guests were, according to Kevin Danaher's *The Year in Ireland*, 'a ring, a small silver coin, a button, a thimble, a chip of wood and a rag'. These were taken as portents of the finder's future:

> The ring meant early marriage, the coin wealth, the button bachelorhood and the thimble spinsterhood, while the chip of wood revealed that the finder would be beaten by the marriage partner, and the rag meant poverty. Some put in a pea and a bean to tell of future poverty and wealth. A little religious medal indicated that the finder would take holy orders or enter a convent.

More recently this custom has been attenuated so that now the normal barmbrack includes only a ring and perhaps a rag or pea. It is easy to imagine that young girls of a hundred or even fifty years ago might take the Hallowe'en divination of the barmbrack very seriously indeed. Entertainment and travel were limited and almost the only hope a young woman had of leaving her parents' home with decency was on the arm of a man, usually one from her own locality.

Particularly in the northern half of Ireland, colcannon (a mixture of mashed potatoes and the seasonal cabbage or kale) and champ (mashed potatoes with milk and onion or shallots) were strongly associated with the dinner or evening meal of Hallowe'en (an association the survival of which is indicated by current supermarket advertising trends). Colcannon was also used for the purpose of marriage divination. The Northern Ireland folklorist Michael J. Murphy describes one such tradition in *At Slieve Gullion's Foot*:

A marriage ring was often mixed in the champ. Here boys and girls gathered round a pot on the floor, and armed with big spoons, tried to be first to get the ring in their mouths. The winner would be married ere next Hallow Eve. This game, however, was most amusing. Little chivalry or decorum was observed in the eagerness to get the ring, and the champ went over hair and eyes and ears as well as into the mouth.

Other means of divination of fate included putting four saucers on the table, one containing a ring, the second water, the third clay and the fourth straw, salt or meal. The participants were led blindfold to the table, where they then placed their hand on one or other of the plates. The ring meant marriage; water indicated that the person would emigrate over the sea; clay meant an early death; and straw, salt or meal, material things, signified wealth.

More specifically, marriage divination with the aim of confirming to the person involved *whom* they would marry was practised extensively at Hallowe'en. No doubt in reality many young women (there is evidence that the majority of the practitioners were women; it was more common for a woman than a man, then, as now, to sigh and pine for a lover) who took part in these traditional, almost pagan-seeming exercises knew right well the name of the man they would like to have as a husband, and the divination was intended to confirm the return of their affection rather than suggest to them future husbands they had yet to dream about.

If a young woman wished to dream of her future partner she would put under her pillow, according to Kevin Danaher, a piece of barmbrack

or the first spoonful of colcannon from the supper dish and the last left on the plate, both put into the girl's left stocking and tied with her right garter, or nine ivy leaves with the words:

Nine ivy leaves I place under my head
to dream of the living and not of the dead,
to dream of the man I am going to wed,
and to see him tonight at the foot of my bed.

She might also go to bed thirsty, having deliberately eaten salty food, so that she might dream about her young man offering her a drink of water. Another inducement to a young man in dreams was for the girl to go to bed with a face washed but not dried. The man would come and offer a towel to dry her face. The theory behind these kinds of strategies seemed to be that the young man would come to supply the deficiencies in the situation of the girl, whether caused by thirst or damp.

Salt was used in a different way in County Down, where the girl would sprinkle it on the four corners of the bed and repeat the following verse, quoted in R. H. Buchanan's *Ulster Folklife*:

> *Salt, salt, I salt thee*
> *In the name of God in unity.*
> *If I'm for a man or a man for me*
> *In my first sleep may I see him,*
> *The colour of his hair, the clothes he'll wear*
> *the day he weds with me.*

A custom that has lingered until this day is that an unmarried girl should sleep with a piece of somebody else's wedding cake under her pillow. If she does this she will dream of the man she will marry in her turn. Obviously this custom was not tied to any period of the year and young women were dependent on another wedding to provide them with the cake. A wedding cake in the modern sense was certainly not a feature of the more humble Irish rural weddings.

The practice of marriage divination at Hallowe'en was associated with several routine activities. A job of housework or farmwork that a girl might do every day was turned into a ritual by being carried out in a certain way or a certain number of times. For instance, when a girl washed the undergarment that was called her shift, she should wring it out on the river bank in the expectation of seeing her lover on the opposite bank, or his reflection in the river water. Another version promised that if she hung her shift out to dry she would see her future partner turning it during the night.

In *Rich and Rare: the Story of Irish Dress*, Bríd Mahon describes how clothes were used in another way to predict a girl's romantic future. 'On Hallowe'en a young unmarried girl would place three knots in her garter and at each knot recite the following incantation:

This knot, this knot, this knot I see
The thing I never saw yet,
To see my love in this array
And what he walks in every day
This night may I in my dreams see,
And if my love be clad in green
His love for me it is well seen,
And if my love be clad in grey
His love for me is far away,
And if my love be clad in blue
His love for me is very true.'

Other means of divination included dropping hair and nail clippings into the fire to bring on a dream of the loved one. A common custom at Hallowe'en, and one that has surivived until recent times, is that of peeling an apple skin in one piece and throwing it over one's shoulder. The peel will take on the shape of the loved one's initial. Similarly, apple peelings thrown into the fire would, it was believed, produce an initial. A girl eating an apple at Hallowe'en while looking into a mirror would see the face of her future husband.

It is only to be expected that such meddling

with the forces of fate or the unseen threads of the future might have frightening consequences, especially at Hallowe'en. Lady Wilde, a folklorist with an appetite for the bizarre and macabre, recounted one such story in *Quaint Irish Customs and Superstitions*. A servant girl eating an apple, as prescribed, with a mirror in her hand, had seen in it what could only be the face of the devil. She fainted with terror, could not be comforted and was found dead the next night 'with her features horribly contorted'.

Marriage divination was also part of the festivities of Shrove. In *Ireland Calendar Customs*, Kevin Danaher observes that Shrove was a household event rather than a public one; eggs in abundance were the basis of the festival food, most notably cooked in pancakes. Marriage divination, where practised, was likewise a family event. Mr and Mrs Hall, who travelled in Ireland in the mid-nineteenth century and reported on what they saw, describe the pancake method of divination in *Ireland, Its Scenery and Character*:

The family group – and the 'boys and girls' of the neighbours – gather round the fireside; and each in turn tries his or her skill in tossing the pancake. The tossing of the first is always allotted to the eldest unmarried daughter of the house, who performs the task not altogether without trepidation, for much of her 'luck' during the year is supposed to depend on her good or ill success on the occasion. She tosses it, and usually so cleverly as to receive it back again without a ruffle in its surface, on its reverse, in the pan. Congratulations upon her fortune go round, and another makes the effort; perhaps this is a sad mischance; the pancake is either not turned or falls among the turf ashes; the unhappy maiden is then doomed – she can have no chance of marrying for a year at least – while the girl who has been lucky is destined to have her 'pick of the boys' as soon as she likes. The cake she has tossed, she is at once called upon to share, and cutting it into as many slices as there are guests, she hands one to each: sometimes the mother's wedding ring has been slipped into the batter out of which the first cake is made, and the person who received the slice in which it is contained is not only the first to be married but is to be doubly lucky in the matter of husband or wife. Men also are permitted to have a chance; and it is a great source of amusement to jog their elbows at the important moment, and so compel them to 'toss the cake crooked'.

From divination – wanting to know who you were going to marry – to making sure that you got the man or woman you wanted is but a short step. Many writers and folklorists describe customs relating to love potions and magic spells, some – including one that involved taking a strip of skin from a corpse while invoking the devil – bordering on black magic. In *Quaint Irish Customs and Superstitions*, Lady Wilde writes:

The country people have still a traditional remembrance of very powerful herbal remedies, and love potions are now frequently in use. They are generally prepared by an old woman; but must be administered by the person who wishes to inspire the tender passion. At the same time, to give a love potion is considered a very awful act as the result may be fatal or at least full of danger.

This account goes on to detail the tragic effects of such a love potion on the mind and spirits of a hitherto-unimpeachable young man.

Lady Wilde gives a recipe for such a potion and directions for other charms to create love in your desired opposite:

Ten leaves of the hemlock dried and powdered and mixed in food or drink will make the person you like to love you in return. Also keep a sprig of mint in your hand till the herb grows moist and warm, then take hold of the hand of the woman you love, and she will follow you as long as the two hands close over the herb. No invocation is necessary; but silence must be kept between the two parties for ten minutes, to give the charm time to work with due success.

Other apparently fail-safe 'secret' ingredients for love potions included the juice of a boiled field-mouse or, in Kerry, the juice of the early purple orchid. With equality for the sexes in mind, a Cork recipe suggests that a girl should boil the excrement of a white gander and give it to drink to the man she had a fancy for; in the opposite case, a young man would win the love of a girl by giving her to drink the boiled excrement of a black chicken.

Whatever the results of divination or love potions, it is certain that in traditional Irish society up to and including the early part of this century the course of true love did not run smooth unless the lovers had the approval of both sets of parents. Relatives or matchmakers arranged marriages that satisfied both family and society, perhaps emphasising less the role of the heart.

2

MATCHMAKING AND DOWRIES

In the days before motorised transport – even after the establishment of the railways, of which people availed mostly for longer journeys – few people in rural Ireland ventured far from home. While a sense of community was so strong that people might know the name of every family in their parish, they might not have any acquaintance with a family of coeval young people from a village six or eight miles away. House or crossroads dances were until the 1920s the only formal entertainment where young people might meet – rambling houses, where people gathered to relay chat, stories and gossip, were mostly the preserve of the older men, women for the most part remaining in their own houses. While many farming families would have a horse or pony for farm work, and it would be put between the shafts of a trap on Sunday to bring the family to Mass, there was no question of this animal being available as a mount for frivolous purposes.

In the nineteenth century and the first half of the twentieth century, rural Ireland was much more densely populated than has since been the case, with most of the population of the country engaged in occupations relating to agriculture. Before the advent of mechanisation, agriculture was very labour-intensive, so that the family and the community had to hold back from emigration the necessary number of workers for the many small farms. Still, the pool of eligible young men or women from which to choose a future partner in life was limited by distance. Older heads were wisely concerned about the danger of in-breeding in such a small community. Consanguinity was a barrier to marriage; even distant relatives – fourth or fifth cousins – were discouraged from marrying each other. Seanchaí Éamon Kelly (b. 1914) relates in his auto-biographical work *The Apprentice* that both his grandfathers, although close friends, were opposed to the marriage of his parents on the ground of consanguinity, although they were only very distantly related.

For the most part dances in dance halls replaced house dances from the 1920s and early 1930s. Enterprising individuals built simple structures of corrugated iron with a wooden frame, a wooden floor and a stage for the musicians. Young people might have a wide range of dance halls to choose from within a ten-mile radius; it was sometimes the case that every village had its own hall.

From this time until the 1950s, the local dance halls thrived. Even though they charged only a penny or two for admission, young people working on their fathers' farms or in service might find even this small sum of money hard to come by – but they managed somehow. Although there was clerical opposition to the dance halls in some areas, just as there had been to house dances and crossroads dances, this seemed to do no harm to them and may even have increased their popularity. Bicycles became more common as the century progressed, although they were still a luxury, and young men could bring their girls home on the bar of their bicycles.

Some of the dance-hall proprietors would play the part of matchmakers, introducing shy young men to equally shy young women and encouraging these retiring people to take the floor so that they would enjoy their visit and come again to their dance halls. Many love matches were entered into as a result of a meeting in one of these dance halls; their heyday also coincided with a gradual relaxation of the hold of the church and their parents over young people.

In any case, Irish society had never been as much anti-romantic as practical. Even in the heyday of the matchmakers there was always plenty of love matches and plenty of courting, with grass flattened along the railway embankment and the hay in farmers' haybarns used for comfort and warmth on cold or rainy mights. If a young man or woman was a suitable partner in every other way, there was no objection to a love match, except perhaps in rare cases where a father was tyrannical or deliberately cruel. Why should there be? Few parents would not rejoice to see their offspring happily settled with the man or woman of their choice. A happy marriage brings more blessings on the couple, on the children of the marriage and on society than does an unhappy one. 'Father came in,' says Sissy O'Brien in *The Farm by Lough Gur*, 'and gave me his blessing. He cared a great deal for my happiness and thought Richard and I were well suited to one another; besides which Richard's land and prospects were on a par with the dowry he would give with me.' Even a man of far less property than Sissy's father might have a similar reaction to a prospective son-in-law, though with lower expectations.

Parents objected to a proposed marriage if the young man or woman in question was not from a suitable background or if a young woman did not bring an adequate dowry with her. Frequently, with most people living humbly by today's standards, it was a case of twopence ha'penny looking down on twopence. The daughter of a small farmer might not be good enough for the son of a comfortable or 'strong' farmer; a small farmer might reject the prospect of a tradesman or cottier – a man without land – as husband for his daughter. Social snobbery was certainly a more threatening factor for young people in love than matchmaking per se. A good dowry made attractive to a man and even more so to his people a woman who might not otherwise be appealing (and not just in terms of physical beauty). Folklore and andecdotes of uncertain provenance make mockery of the man who marries for money and lives to regret it:

> The dowry drops over the cliff but the drooping lip remains on the wife.

> If you marry money the woman will outlast it.

Another consequence of made marriages was elopement or 'runaway' marriages. If a couple were thwarted in their love – which might happen if, for instance, the parents intended the young woman for a more prosperous but older and less handsome husband – she might elope with the young man. Couples also wedded secretly in order that their parents might know only when that marriage was a *fait accompli*: if the couple was considered too young or if they lacked the means to get married, in the opinion of their parents. One young man who eloped was Paddy 'the Cope' Gallagher, the Donegalman who founded the cooperative at Templecrone. He describes it in his autobiographical *My Story*:

> Sally and I decided to get married but we did not want our parents to know it; I especially, as I should not leave them for another few years as my earnings were badly wanted at home. We got married on a Sunday sevening in Dungloe.

Matchmakers who were motivated by the desire to see deserving people suitably married and by a respect for tradition and social order were highly regarded in Irish society. Matchmaking was rarely a full-time occupation but it was a source of income, either in cash or in kind. There were certain to have been some matchmakers who were motivated purely by avarice but it is hard to imagine such individuals being successful at the trade of matchmaking in the long term.

Matchmaking was a job that could be successfully performed by both men and women, a woman matchmaker putting emphasis on the feminine, wifely qualities of the woman for whom she was arranging a marriage. Matchmakers usually operated unofficially. A matchmaker might be the woman or man who ran the shop or post office or the local pub; he might just as easily be an ordinary farmer with an interest in the affairs of other people. Obviously people who were in the way of meeting the public at large were more likely to be successful matchmakers than those on remote farmsteads, although if a man or woman had a reputation as a wise and trustworthy matchmaker, distance was no object for those who wished to avail of their services. In one of the stories in *Ireland's Master Storyteller*, Éamon Kelly describes how one Kerry match was made:

> The other two girls got married, he had no trouble getting rid of 'em, but there was no demand for Nell on account of she couldn't talk . . . There was a huckster's shop at the side of the road, and a

very knowledgeable woman at the head of it; she had the name of bringing many a happy couple together. Casey [the father] used to get the small things there. He'd get the big groceries in town. He was in the shop one day and he said to the little woman if she could at all to be on the lookout for a suitable partner for Nell [the daughter]. She said she would. Who should call into the shop the following day but Jeremiah O'Sullivan that lived a few miles up, and when she was papering up the few commands for him the little woman said, 'How long is your wife dead now, Jeremiah?'

Kelly's view of the matchmaker is benign, in this story and in his work in general, but this is in keeping with his view of life in general: in his works, people are foolish, snobbish, cowardly or vain but rarely mean or malicious. A much darker view of the matchmaker features in Kerry playwright John B. Keane's fine but dark and tragic play *Sive*, which was first performed in 1959:

The door opens slowly and a man peers cautiously about the kitchen. He wears a disfigured felt hat upon unruly hair and looks as if he had not shaved for a week. He is shifty-looking, ever on his guard. He is fortyish . . . He is Thomasheen Seán Rua, a matchmaker.

The majority of 'made' marriages seem to have been arranged not by a matchmaker but by the family or friends of a young couple. This would certainly be the case if the young couple knew and liked each other already. A cousin or a friend of the young man, for instance, might visit the girl's home and mention the possibility of an alliance between the two. A favourite time for such opening moves, according to Kevin Danaher, was 'between the two Christmases', that is between Christmas Day and the Epiphany or 'Women's Christmas' on 6 January.

Once the initial introduction was over, the two parties needed to come to an agreement. The fathers of the young woman and the young man did the serious negotiation and the main sticking point was naturally the dowry. Once that was agreed in principle, a ceremony known as 'eating the gander' took place in the house of the bride-to-be. This was the occasion for the young couple to get to know each other if they did not already, and to decide whether they liked the look of each other or not. Many couples would, of course, already have an understanding. If the young man was marrying into a farm this would be the opportunity for him to walk the land and count the cows and other animals kept there. A celebratory meal of goose, male or female, was served, and often a long night of music, singing and dancing ensued. During the course of the evening, the final discussion of the legal arrangements for the marriage and the transfer of ownership of the farm (if applicable) occurred and the way was cleared for the signing of the legal agreements between the two parties, the 'bindings' as they were called. These were sometimes signed on the same evening the gander was eaten but it was more often the case that they were signed in the presence of a solicitor in the nearest town. The dowry, if it was in cash, was also entrusted to the care of the solicitor on this occasion.

In Ireland before the Great Famine of 1845–51, the land of the poor was subdivided into smaller and smaller subsistence patches, on which it was possible to grow only potatoes. If a peasant farmer had five children he would divide his own acre between them; each would get married, build a *bothán* (hut) and get on with the business of subsistence. After the great calamity of the Famine – caused in part by this system of potato monoculture on tiny patches of land – and the death or emigration of a large proportion of the population, holdings were consolidated. The farm would be left to one son while the other sons found work if possible or, more likely, emigrated to Britain or America. The daughters would go into service, emigrate, or, if by good fortune a dowry could be found, 'marry into' another farm.

A dowry (*spré*) was then always required of any girl who married into a farm. The bigger the farm, the more she had to bring in terms of money, cows or other goods. The details would be hammered out, perhaps initially by a matchmaker and then by the fathers of the bride and groom, eventually being put into legal language, as described above. If there were no other calls on it, the dowry would be used to improve the farm or increase its size or to acquire stock or implements. Once the woman married she had no further rights to what she had brought with her into the house.

If a farmer had only a daughter or daughters, he looked for a young man for the eldest, a *cliamhain isteach*, to marry in. If the girl's farm was a substantial and prosperous one, he too would be required to bring a 'portion' in money or stock. However, a young man with a reputation for steadiness and industry would have something to recommend him as a son-in-law and the financial demands on him might be less.

Dowries could be paid in cash or in cattle. They were not always supplied by the family of the bride. Sometimes the young woman herself worked in service at home or emigrated to America for a period, earning enough to pay her way into a small farm on her return. The money was often not touched by the groom or his family but was used instead as a dowry to make a match for a daughter of the house in turn. The dowry might later be used by *her* groom to settle on his sister. Éamon Kelly describes the domino effect of an 'American' dowry that might have been considered substantial at the time:

A lot of young people going away at that time looked upon America as a place or state of punishment where some people suffered for a time before they came home and bought a pub or a farm or married into land or business . . . like Pegg's Yank. A fair amount succeeded. If you walked around the country forty years ago every second house you'd go into either the man or his wife had been to America.

Many is the young woman came back – well she wouldn't be young then after ten years in New York, but young enough! – and married a farmer, bringing with her a fortune of three or four hundred dollars. Then, if the farmer had an idle sister – and by idle there I don't mean out of work! – the fortune was for her. Then she could marry another farmer, or the man of her fancy, that's how the system worked, and that fortune might take another idle sister out of that house, and so on! So that the same three hundred dollars earned hard running up and down the steps of high stoop houses in New York city could be the means of getting anything up to a dozen women under the blankets here in Ireland! And all pure legal!

Kelly spins a yarn about himself being matched with a young girl of the locality: a match that never came to fruition because of a comical error. As a *cliamhain isteach* or 'marrying in' man, he, although a tradesman and a good prospect, would have to put up seventy pounds, a lot of money in the 1930s. That some people had the habit of paying the dowry in instalments is indicated by his future father-in-law's brusque remark: 'And there'll be no twenty pounds down and the rest at the first christening! A lump sum or nothing.'

Were matchmakers a useful institution? Was the matchmaking system misused by tyrannical or avaricious parents? Were 'made' marriages less happy than love matches? As no research was done at the time, it is difficult to answer these questions with any degree of assurance. Obviously, matchmakers and made marriages were products of their time, and their time, by and large, is past. (An exception is the September end-of-season matchmaking festival in Lisdoonvarna, County Clare.)

At its worst, the concept of matchmaking conjures up the image of the schoolgirl Sive in John B. Keane's play of that name, rushing out of the house to her death in a bog rather than be forced into an arranged marriage with the ageing Seán Dóta when she loves instead a young man called Liam. Here is how that potential husband is described by the matchmaker himself, in an effort to be complimentary:

> But he's a hardy thief with the mad mind for women breaking out through him like the tetter with no cure for it. What matter if he is as grey as a goat. There is many a young man after a year of marriage losing his heart for love-making. This man have the temper. He would swim the Shannon for a young wife. He would

spoil her, I tell you. There is good reward
for all concerned in it.

This is to be a commercial transaction. Many
matchmakers were not motivated by avarice;
Thomasheen Seán Rua is. He offers Mena, Sive's
cold and hard-hearted aunt, '200 sovereigns for
you if the girl will consent.' Like all those of low
principles, she is quick to be suspicious: 'And
what is in it for you? It isn't out of the goodness
of yeer heart you are playing your hand.' He
replies, 'There will be 100 pounds for me.'

No doubt some young men and women like
the unfortunate Sive were at times treated
harshly, when economic interests outweighed
any consideration of compatibility – for example
in age – never mind romance. Anecdotal evidence, most of it from the older generation –
people who might still have a sneaking regard
for the matchmaker's methods – is that made
marriages were, on the whole, successful. Since
there was until recently very little overt evidence
of marital breakdown in Irish society, particularly
in rural society, it is not possible to extrapolate
contentment from the absence of such break-

down. There must have been many women in loveless marriages who were deprived of any economic independence (apart from the paltry amounts of egg money they might earn; fowl were traditionally women's business) and who lived only for their children.

On the other hand, made matches were often the only way that people past the first flush of youth could be put in touch with a suitable partner: the shy bachelor from the remote hilly farm who waited until he was thirty-five and the death of his mother had made space (and created necessity) for another woman in the house; the spinster who returned from fifteen years of service in New York with a tidy dowry but few prospects of attracting a suitable (genuine) man. Romance comes naturally to the young, given the slimmest opportunity, but not so easily later on, or to widowers, or to those, in Yeats's words, 'not entirely beautiful'.

My personal view is that since, to paraphrase the words (in *Pride and Prejudice*) of that greatest of writers on the institution of marriage, Jane Austen, happiness in marriage is entirely a matter of chance, made marriages had just as much chance of succeeding as marriages of inclination. Many a marriage that started with true love ended badly; many a couple that began almost as strangers ended up happy. The available evidence, in any case, suggests that inclination and prudence often coincided.

3

SHROVETIME AND CHALK SUNDAY

'And at last, when November was going out in dreary darkness, came the day of my marriage,' begins the account of her wedding day by Sissy O'Brien, the narrator of *The Farm by Lough Gur*. This late-nineteenth-century wedding between the daughter of a prosperous County Limerick farmer and Richard Fogarty, another prosperous local farmer, was untypical in many ways of the customs of the time – and certainly so in the date the family chose for its celebration. Not all Irish marriages took place in Shrovetime – the period immediately before Lent, with Shrove Tuesday itself the most popular and auspicious day of all – but the vast majority of traditional marriages among ordinary (mostly poor) rural people did. The tradition of hundreds of years rather than any strict ecclesiastical ruling decreed that it was not permissible to marry during Lent. It was therefore necessary to marry outside of Lent. Over time it came to pass that nobody got married *after* Lent; all weddings took place before Lent, in Shrovetime.

Shrove Tuesday, the day before the start of Lent and, like that period of penance, a movable feast, coincides roughly with the manifestation of spring. Shrove Tuesday and the days immediately preceding it are days of carnival in many countries in Europe and South America. Where Lent was observed, so too was the festival that preceded it.

As has happened in many such cases, the beliefs and customs of the people were supported and therefore solidified by the pattern of agricultural work in Ireland. Winter was a time of little work and greater leisure for – among other activities – courting and matchmaking. The wedding safely out of the way in February or March, the year's work on the farm could begin, the bride (or, less often, the groom) who 'married in' contributing another pair of hands to the agricultural labours. Traditionally, the sowing of crops like potatoes began in the days or week preceding St Patrick's Day, 17 March – as early a date as the waterlogged soil, caused by mainly wet winters, particularly in the western counties of Ireland, would allow.

The tradition of Shrove weddings was almost universal in rural Ireland in the nineteenth century and well into the twentieth century. It died, along with many other folk customs, with the advent of mass communication and easier travel.

As tradition dictated that people should marry at Shrove, those who failed to find themselves a partner, particularly those who repeatedly offended and were in danger of ending up as spinsters or bachelors, were reminded of the disapproval of the community on 'Chalk Sunday', the first Sunday of Lent. The clothes of the unmarried were marked by pieces of chalk, children and mischievous young people being the usual perpetrators. Most people seemed to take this public scapegoating in good part, as it was doled out without fear or favour on this Sunday every year. According to Kevin Danaher, this tradition was widespread in the southern half of Ireland throughout the nineteenth century and continued on in some places into the twentieth century. In a few areas, Chalk Sunday fell on the Sunday before Shrove Tuesday instead of the first Sunday of Lent, so that the people whose clothes were marked might still have time to cobble a match together before the Shrove Tuesday deadline. 'There was no knowing the amount of people that'd get married at that time between Chalk Sunday and Shrove Tuesday,' according to Éamon Kelly.

The island monastery of Sceilg Mhichíl, beautifully but inaccessibly situated off the coast of south Kerry, was home to a community of monks until after 1000 AD (there are records of the deaths of monks there in 950 and 1044). As the island was so cut off from the mainland, it was difficult to impose church discipline and dates on the community there. It is not clear why, but the tradition grew up that on the Skellig, as it was called, Easter was celebrated a month later than on the mainland. This tradition was perhaps a legacy of the controversy about the date of Easter that erupted in the Irish Church at the time of the Synod of Whitby (664 AD), when Rome attempted to impose on the Christian world a uniform means of calculating the date of Easter. The Skellig idea was merely another way for the community to exert pressure on people to get married: if they could not get married in the ordinary way, having missed the Shrove Tuesday deadline, they might in theory still be married on the Skellig. According to Kevin Danaher, the unmarried were mocked in the early days of Lent by having 'You're off to the Rock, I suppose?' or 'Don't miss the boat!' shouted at them as they passed in a public place. It would not have been surprising if those who missed making a match stayed at home in bed for the first week of Lent.

Joe Dinneen, a poet from the Sliabh Luachra area on the Cork–Kerry border and a brother of the lexicographer An tAthair Pádraig Ua Duinnín, specialised in the composition of Skelligs lists. One of these is quoted in Donal Hickey's book about Sliabh Luachra, *Stone Mad for Music*:

> *John Dan Jack we won't let back, although*
> *   he is but a pet,*
> *He is the first and not the worst to give the*
> *   boys a wet,*

Miss Buckley fair, abiding near, controls his
    senses now,
He'll bring her home, she'll be his own, in
    gold-crowned Moulagow.

In one of his stories, Éamon Kelly also quotes
a Skellig list:

If you weren't married by Shrove Tuesday
night you could throw your hat at it.
You'd have to wait another twelve months,
unless you went out to Skelligs, where
the monks kept old time. Indeed a
broadsheet used to come out called the
Skelligs List – it used be shoved under
the doors Ash Wednesday morning. Oh,
a scurrilous document in verse lampoon-
ing all those bachelors who should have,
but didn't, get married during Shrovetime.

There's Mary the Bridge
And Johnny her boyfriend,
They are walking out now
For twenty-one springs!
There's no ditch nor no dyke

That they haven't rolled in –
She must know by now
The nature of things!
'Oh, Johnny,' says she,
'Do you think we should marry
And put an end for all time
To this fooster and fuss?'
'Ah, Mary,' says he,
'You must be near doting.
Who do you think
Would marry either of us!'

In some parts of Cork and Kerry, these Skellig poems were printed in large numbers and sold widely. They were usually anonymous and sometimes aroused strong but impotent anger in the people they targeted. Another custom practised more recently was for a list of suitable couples, purporting to be a schedule of those participating in a 'grand excursion' by boat to the Skellig, to be hung in a public place.

So anxious was the community to discourage bachelorhood and spinsterhood that a whole range of other activities existed in different parts of the country to single out those who should have married but did not do so. In the west of Ireland there was a custom that salt was sprinkled on bachelors and spinsters to preserve them against the next Shrove. At Ballinrobe in County Mayo this was carried out on the first Monday in Lent, known as 'Salt Monday'.

Men who had repeatedly resisted attempts to make a match for them and were in danger of becoming hardened bachelors were singled out for particular abuse. Practical jokes were played on them and young men of the locality sang ditties outside their door to the accompaniment of loud noises.

4

THE BOTTOM DRAWER

In *Forgetting Frolic*, Linda May Ballard gives an account of the necessary preparations for a traditional nineteenth-century marriage. They include assembling a bottom drawer of household linens, including a christening robe and a winding sheet for laying out a body.

The wealthy could buy complete sets of the finest household linen from shops like Harrods, if necessary by mail order. The same was true of the trousseau, the collection of personal linens that a young woman should have for her new life: pettocoats, camisoles, corsets and all the rest. Smart shops in London, Belfast, Dublin and Cork did a thriving trade for those who could afford it.

A patchwork quilt was also a traditional item in a bottom drawer. It appears that all over the country, sewing and lining a patchword quilt was a communal activity. This is Éamon Kelly's description in *Ireland's Master Storyteller* of a quilting session in preparation for the marriage of a young bride:

> In my father's time, when a young woman was getting married, the other women of around her own age would come to her house one night, bringing with them materials to make a patchwork quilt, and this quilt when it was made was a present for the young wife to bring to her new home.
>
> They had a quilting frame that time on which to stretch the base and cover of the new quilt. Then one clever lady with an eye for design would take a splinter from the fire, let the burnt end cool, and with this draw out the shapes on the cover. Each woman was given a section to work at, and she'd take out the odds and ends of coloured materials, cutting them in various shapes according to fancy while the supervising lady moved the

pieces around to get a nice balance of colour and so on.

As the women sewed up and down, they'd put a lot of packing between the base and the cover, bits and scraps of worn garments, a piece of an old woollen drawers, anything there was heat in. And when they were finished, some of those quilts were so heavy you'd nearly want to get artificial respiration after coming out from under them.

There would be great jollity among the women as they worked and talked of comical and strange happenings, and talk of courting and talk of love, for it was Shrovetime and matrimony was in the air.

For the majority of Irish women, both bottom drawer and trousseau were humble affairs. They would have a patchwork quilt pieced together by relatives and neighbouring women, some basic linen and two outfits, one for every day, one for Sunday – and that would almost certainly be the outfit in which they had been married. What

Eilís Ní Shúilleabháin writes about her wedding purchases in *Letters from the Great Blasket* would certainly not have been untypical.

> All my friends here gave me every help for my wedding, only for them I would have a great trouble to make up the deficit. So it was very hard as every thing in town is as expensive as it could be, but now thank God it's over.

Society in the nineteenth century and the first part of the twentieth was full of striking contrasts and inequality. Marriage exposed these inequalities. This is Sissy O'Brien in *The Farm by Lough Gur*:

> In my petticoats, white stockings and satin slippers, I went to mother in the spare room to put on the dress which Bessie had worn at her wedding, white, soft and lacey, and her narrow wreath of orange-blossom, and the Limerick-lace veil lent me by Mr Todd of Limerick. I took my gloves in my hand and let

mother wrap my shivering body in a
shawl and a fluffy new blanket.

Like Sissy O'Brien, a nineteenth- or early-
twentieth-century bride from a prosperous family
might be every inch the romantic ideal, clothed
in white silk, satin and lace. Her gown might
be a family heirloom (rather as christening robes
sometimes are), perhaps worn already by her
mother, aunt or sister. For the majority of young
women, however, such splendour was incon-
ceivable. It was probably not even coveted until
the 1930s and not widespread until after the
Second World War. In the 1950s, newspapers
and magazines brought images of princesses
(such as Margaret and Grace) and film stars.
From this time on a distinctive white (or *à la
rigueur* pale cream or ivory) dress with veil or
headdress became the 'traditional' wedding attire
for women, many brides probably not realising
how short-lived the tradition is for all except the
wealthiest classes of society. Whether the style be
ballerina, empire, Victorian, 1920s or 'modern', a
distinguishing feature of contemporary bridal attire
is that it is bought, often at great expense, for the

wedding day, and nobody expects the bride to wear it again. Indeed, a second outfit, called the 'going away', is normally procured and worn for leaving on honeymoon. This outfit is of more practical use in the months after the wedding.

Traditionally, most Irish women did not have a great deal of money to spend on wedding clothes. In some ways weddings were much less elaborate than they are now; although the celebrations may have lasted longer and more alcohol may have been consumed, there was certainly much less expenditure, if one takes into account all that is currently spent on flowers, photographers and honeymoons. The normal wedding attire was a frock or suit, which may or may not have been new for the occasion and which would certainly be expected to be put to good use for long after the wedding day. Eilís Ní Shúilleabháin wore 'a blue dress with white collar and cuffs, a long one too, a pair of black shoes, and a new shawl'. Her woman companion dressed identically. Suits became popular wedding attire in the towns: they could be in any colour but pastels such as pale blue and lilac were preferred. In rural Ireland men wore their best suit; if a new suit was bought for the wedding, it would certainly be worn for a long time to come.

The Ulster Folk and Transport Museum, which is situated in Cultra, County Down, contains a fine selection of nineteenth-century wedding gowns, from various strata of society. In *Forgetting Frolic*, Linda May Ballard describes wedding dresses of the 1850s: silk fabric in various serviceable colours such as brown and purple with the crinolines of the day. It is obvious that these dresses were going to be taken out again and again for 'good' wear.

Guests at a wedding in rural Ireland in the nineteenth century or the early part of the twentieth century would not be dressed as expensively or elaborately as at a similar ceremony today. It would not have been possible for most people to acquire a new outfit or even a new pair of shoes for a wedding.

5

BRIGHTLY DAWNS
OUR WEDDING DAY

Until the mid-nineteenth century Irish marriages
were normally celebrated at home, usually in the
groom's house, if it was here that the couple
were going to live, but occasionally in the bride's
family home, if the young man was marrying in
there. It is thought that this custom dated from
the days of the Penal Laws, when Catholics
were forbidden to worship in public. Later on,
it was possible (and still is possible) to have a
wedding at home by special licence but from the
late nineteenth century onwards, only the wealthy
chose to do this.

Kevin Danaher's *In Ireland Long Ago* provides
a lively description of a traditional nineteenth-
century wedding taking place in the groom's
home. From the morning time, people would

converge on the house; at least one representative of each family in the community would attend because to fail to do so would be a serious insult to the bride and groom. The bride's party would travel from her house to the groom's in traps or carts, or on horseback, the bride riding pillion with her father or brother. Sometimes so many people came to the wedding that the modest farmhouse kitchen was not big enough to accommodate all of them. The overflow had to be put in the barn. (Since almost all weddings took place in February or March, the weather would not have been appropriate for a garden party.) It was essential for the family hosting the celebration to have *togha agus rogha*, an ample sufficiency of food and drink, or they would be scorned for generations in the parish. For this reason, and because people in general had modest means, it was not unknown for kindly neighbours to make discreet contributions on the day – of fowl, meat, drink or cakes.

The eating, drinking and general enjoyment would begin before the ceremony proper. After the priest arrived (on horseback) and married the couple in the kitchen in view of as many of the community as could crowd in there, joy would be unconfined. The priest was expected to partake of the food and drink and even sing a song or play a tune on an instrument if he had the talent. The he would leave, often to perform another wedding: if it was Shrove Tuesday he might have three or four to perform in different parts of the parish, and by the time he arrived at the last of them, it would be well on in the evening.

As the nineteenth century progressed the wedding ceremony itself began to take place in the local church. The bride's party and the groom's party would make their way separately, using whatever means of conveyance they could call on. Then they and the large number of guests would make their way to the groom's (or if appropriate the bride's) house and the rest of the celebration would be as before. Kevin Danaher describes in his book *In Ireland Long Ago* a country wedding that took place in 1921, when he saw eight horse-drawn vehicles coming back from the church to the bride's parents' house: six traps, a back-to-back and a side-car.

Although a great deal of drink was consumed

over the day and night (and perhaps into a second day) of the wedding, it was considered insulting to the bride and groom for any guest to be overtly or offensively drunk. Different members of the hosting family, brothers or relatives of the groom, kept order, dispensed the drink or acted as compères for the entertainment, calling on a singer here, a step-dancer there, to give of their best, and making sure that the fiddlers or accordeon-players were kept well lubricated.

Music and dance were always part of the celebration. For people who were used to the idea of house dances and who would always know a good musician who would oblige with his fiddle or accordeon, dancing was a natural progression from eating and drinking. Polka and other sets would be danced, children would take the floor for step dancing, and those with fine voices from among the family and neighbours would be induced to sing a traditional song or two. Eilís Ní Shúilleabháin, author of *Letters from the Great Blasket,* describes her own humble wedding: 'We went to town again and had breakfast in Keane's house and done lots of messages there too and Seán was playing the violin and we all enjoyed the evening until rather late.'

Tradition decreed that neither bride nor groom should sing at their own wedding. They should, however, dance the first dance, along with the best man and bridesmaid.

Many superstitions attached themselves to the wedding day, as one might expect of an event on which people's future happiness depended. A fine day was a good omen: a wet day presaged a gloomy life of hardship. Saturday was an unlucky day to marry; green was an unlucky colour for a bridal gown, as was the wearing of pearls as an adornment by the bride. A popular saying, quoted by Bríd Mahon in *Rich and Rare: the Story of Irish Dress*, went:

> *Married in blue, you're sure to rue,*
> *Married in grey, you'll go far away,*
> *Married in yellow, ashamed of your fellow,*
> *Married in brown, you'll live out of town,*
> *Married in white, you'll be all right,*
> *Married in red, you'll wish yourself dead,*
> *Married in green, not fit to be seen.*

It was said that a couple that married in harvest time would spend all their lives gathering. A man rather than a woman should be the first to wish the bride joy. It was lucky for the bridal cortège to meet a cuckoo (hardly likely in Shrovetime) or three magpies. For the wedding party to meet a funeral was a very bad omen so care was taken to choose an alternative route if a funeral was making its way to the graveyard on the day of the wedding.

In *Superstitions of the Irish County People*, Padraic O'Farrell mentions a marriage tradition that was beautiful in both the material and spiritual senses:

> The groom presented his bride with some newly churned country butter beside a mill, a tree or a stream – all symbols of endurance. He recited a prayer that went:

> *Oh woman, loved by me, mayest thou give me thy heart, thy soul and body.*

Tradition (still observed) also decreed that the bride should not see the groom on the morning of the wedding until she met him at the ceremony. 'I did not go in with John [her husband-to-be] at all, because it is said here around in every place that it is unlucky to go with him in the motor car to the church,' wrote Eilís Ní Shúilleabháin.

A wedding was a time to show off to the neighbours if any refinement had been added to your house or if you were able to provide food not normally enjoyed in those parts. Éamon Kelly describes one wedding's comestibles (or combustibles, as he likes to call them) thus:

> In Haley's house the wedding was, and people who were there told me it was a fine turn-out. No expense spared, this and that there, currany tops and what- not, all kinds of grudles, buns, trifle and that shaky shivery stuff you'd ate with a spoon.

> The wedding went on all night, into the following day as long as the drink held out!

Not alone were there music, recitation, singing and dancing a-plenty but later in the evening when spirits were high after a fair amount of drink had been consumed, the young men of the party might begin to play other more boisterous games. One such game, called 'Kick the Turnip' and involving just that activity, features in another account of a wedding by Éamon Kelly:

> No shortage of anything. Plenty of food and drink, and out in the night when they had enough of the Highland Fling and the Kerry Victoria, enough singing and reciting, a lot of the lads there had a good cargo on board, and one of them suggested why not play the game called 'Kick the Turnip', which was common in that quarter. And how the game was played was, you'd get a sizeable turnip and cut a channel around the equator. You'd tie a rope into that and at the other end of the rope you'd put a similar weight, maybe another turnip. You'd throw it over the collar-brace and then you could adjust the turnip up or down, a foot from

the ground or whatever you wanted. And the man that'd win the game'd be the man that'd tip the turnip with the top of his toecap and it the highest from the ground.

Wedding breakfasts were not expected to end for twenty-four hours. It was a great source of pride for the hosts at a wedding to say that they had danced until daylight. During this time, the newly-weds might need a little privacy so they slipped upstairs or put a chest-of-drawers in front of a downstairs door. This did not give rise to any adverse comment; what was natural was entirely accepted.

In many parts of the country the wedding was not complete without the visit of the strawboys, or 'soppers' as they were also called. Late on in the evening when the merriment was at its peak, a group of six or eight young local men, with one men acting as leader, would call without invitation at the wedding house – uninvited but not unwelcome for it would be a churlish host who would refuse entry to them. The groom or his father would issue an invitation to them on the threshold. They were dressed in garments of straw with a conical straw hat and straw mask on their faces. The leader would go to the bride and wish her joy, then invite her to dance. He and three others of his company, partnered by the bridesmaids or sisters of the bride would then take the floor in an eight-hand reel or, in other parts of the country, a polka set.

Although the strawboys were in disguise, part of the fun of the wedding, especially for the young women, was to guess their identity by pulling the straw masks from their faces or recognising the clothes they were wearing (usually not their own clothes but garments 'borrowed', usually without permission, from members of their families or relatives). The leader of the strawboys would then instruct one of his group to sing or step-dance, for one of the qualifications for being selected as a strawboy was the ability to perform in some way – or if members of the group were identified, one of the wedding party might call on them to do a party piece. The strawboy interlude ended with drinks all round and the visitors left, often to go on to the next wedding, as Shrovetime was the popular time for weddings. On Shrove Tuesday itself, several goups of strawboys would do the rounds in a parish and more than one group of strawboys might visit each wedding.

Kevin Danaher in his book *In Ireland Long Ago* writes that the custom of dressing in straw had come to an end in his area (County Limerick) and that the group, called 'soppers' in his time and place, would be more likely to be disguised by wearing old clothes and blackening their faces with soot. But in Éamon Kelly's autobiographical *The Apprentice*, the author describes how he himself was part of a group disguised partly with straw, in County Kerry around 1930. The group, more equitably, was made up of three girls and three boys. He had thought of the idea of going 'strawing', as it was called, in order to spend time with the girl he loved, Jude:

Some evenings before, we came together and with wisps of straw made ropes to put around our lower legs like army puttees. We fashioned bands of straw to place about the waist and shoulders and plaited shorter lengths to decorate our caps. We, the men, turned our coats inside out and the girls, borrowing their fathers' or their brothers' coats, did the same thing. With the straw leggings on and our bodies festooned in straw and our faces covered in pieces of old lace curtain, we defied anyone to recognise us.

When they arrived at the wedding house, their captain knocked on the door and chanted:

> *Strawboys on the threshold,*
> *Strawboys at the door.*
> *Keep a place for strawboys*
> *On the dancing floor.*
> *We wish the bride and groom*
> *The very best of cheer.*
> *May they have a son or daughter*
> *Ere the end of the year.*

The strawboys accepted a drink and danced and sang, remaining incognito despite the best efforts of some of the guests to reveal their identity. As they were leaving, they witnessed a strawboy fight between the group that had succeeded them and a third group that was refused admittance by the man of the house. Whatever the laws of hospitality, this particular Mr Galvin of the Knob obviously thought that enough was enough.

Kevin Danaher documents in *The Year in Ireland* a custom that existed among prosperous farmers of the Golden Vale (the area of Munster comprising the fertile land of north Cork, north Kerry, east Limerick and part of Tipperary) and probably had its origin in England. When the newly married couple came out of the church:

> The groom was handed a dish or tray containing some handfuls of copper and small silver coints, which he threw into the air to scatter among the crowd, where children and others scrambled for them. In former times numbers of beggars and tramps assembled for this occasion and sometimes quarrels and brawls occurred between them.

Sissy O'Brien and her new husband Richard Fogarty in *The Farm by Lough Gur* certainly belong to the class of prosperous farmers who give money away to the poor on their wedding day, although in their case they wait until they are about to begin their honeymoon journey:

> We arrive at Harris's Hotel, Knocklong, and step into a throng of beggars, not our own, but pushing, vociferous creatures from Limerick. Richard throws them coppers which the waiter has in readiness at the door; he knows the etiquette of weddings.

As the twentieth century wore on, however, and old traditions gradually waned and died, the traditional wedding too declined in popularity. By the time of the Second World War the bridal party was likely to celebrate a wedding 'breakfast' in a nearby hostelry or in a hotel in the local town. Some cars would be available by then, and the local hackney driver would convey the bride to the church and the bridal party to the reception. The church wedding was early and the proceedings, devoid of any singing or dancing, would be over by the middle the day. It was not until the 1960s in rural Ireland that couples started to have what quickly seemed like 'traditional' weddings: a long white dress and all the trimmings, a photographer and a reception that lasted until late in the night, complete with musicians and singers. It is ironic that at some of these modern receptions, the old country dances, particularly the polka set, have been revived and, as in the house weddings of long ago, a great deal of drink is likely to be consumed.

6

AFTER THE BALL IS OVER

It is clear from folklore and written sources that few Irish couples until relatively recent times went on a honeymoon or wedding journey. If a railway station was within easy reach – and the rail network in the west and south of Ireland was much more extensive at the end of the nineteenth century than it is now – it was certainly possible to make a trip to a city like Cork or Galway or to a seaside location like Kilkee in County Clare. However, the fact that almost all marriages took place in February or March would have made the idea of travel for pleasure less attractive. In any case it was simply not part of the custom in rural Ireland. Weddings were enjoyed by the participants, their families, relatives and by many members of the larger community or parish. It is certain that they were seen as community celabrations and not as private, hole-and-corner affairs. But when the day and night, or days and nights, of drinking, singing and dancing were over, it was nose to the grindstone for the new groom on his own smallholding and the new bride, who had to make the adjustment to the household and farm labours of her new life. Eilís Ní Shúilleabháin, who lived on the Great Blasket Island off the west coast of County Kerry and describes her life in *Letters from the Great Blasket*, got married in Ballyferriter Church on the mainland and 'was in my little island home then again at about nine o'clock Saturday night.'

One of Éamon Kelly's stories in *Ireland's Master Storyteller* makes reference to a honeymoon as something that 'made history':

Why then I heard of a woman that married a blacksmith, and what's more she came all the way back from America to marry him. He was a good mark for as well as the forge he had a nice bit of land with a good house on it. There was no out and out great love between them, just that he had an empty house and she was tired of America. They got married, a made match, and they made history for they were the first couple from that part of the world to go away on a honeymoon. When they got off the train above in Glanmire station in Cork she says to him, 'They are all looking at us. They know very well that we are fresh from the altar! Is there anything I could do,' says she, 'to make it appear as if we are a couple of years married?'

'Of course there is,' he said. 'Catch hold of the bag and walk on in front of me!'

The norm was the couple called Haley and Nonie, who had a very fine and lengthy wedding celebration indeed, one enjoyed by a great number of people in their parish. But 'when all the 'goodbyes' were said, and all the relations gone, Haley and Nonie milked the cows and went to bed!'

On the other hand, couples from higher strata of society, who could use hired labour to do the work of house or farm and had more money to spare for amusement, were able to afford the indulgence of a wedding journey. In *The Farm by Lough Gur*, Sissy O'Brien, like any girl of her class in England, does have a honeymoon – in London: 'Richard and I drive away in the landau. We are going to Knocklong because of catching the Dublin train.'

There was a tradition that neither the bride nor her new husband should enter the bride's home until a month had elapsed from the wedding day; the exception being those homes where the man had 'married in'. It may have served as a precaution against young women 'running home to mother' if everything in the new marriage was not entirely to their liking.

Apart from inclination or disinclination, and excluding altogether any thoughts of romance, marriage carried with it certain social advantages, especially for women. In an era before education or careers for women were the norm, almost all women would have aspired to marriage and bearing children. Society would have supported the desirability of this outcome. (It could be argued that even today, when so much in society has changed, 'catching' a man is still considered an achievement for certain women.) 'It is funny being engaged,' ponders Sissy O'Brien in *The Farm by Lough Gur:*

> One feels like plain gingerbread suddenly gilt; parents are pleased, as if one had won a race; sisters assume an unusual respect. One does not quite know how an engaged girl ought to behave.

A rural Irishwoman of any era up to the middle of this century would certainly have to work hard in the house and on the farm and to tend to her children as they arrived, but she gained in status by being mistress of her own house – and by being associated with the home, farm or other property of her new husband even if she had no legal rights over it – rather than just a daughter or sister in her family of origin. If she was lucky and her husband was kind and generous in sharing the small proceeds of the farm they worked together, she might revel in her status of matron, looking with pity or contempt on the unmarried spinster of thirty-five. Many women, however, found that their marriages were far from being a bed of roses. Even if they were allowed to marry the man for whom they felt an inclination rather than being matched with an ageing bachelor for the sake of his farm, they might find before them in their marital home an elderly mother-in-law or father-in-law or both, and perhaps a spinster sister or bachelor brother of their husband, who had not the financial means to set up a home of their own. Conflicts between new wife and mother-in-law feature frequently in both humorous and tragic vein.

In her autobiography *Peig* (translated by Bryan MacMahon), Peig Sayers describes how her brother Seán makes a match for her with a man from the Great Blasket Island, Pádraig Ó Guithín. They meet for the first time only a few days before their wedding but Peig decides that marriage with him is the best option for her. In the first place, she has great confidence in the brother who arranged the match but more importantly:

I considered for a while for I had two chances in the palm of my hand – to marry or go into service again. I was sick

and tired of that same service and I
thought it would be better for me to have
a man to my back and someone to protect
me, and to own a house too, where I
could sit down at my ease whenever I'd
be weary.

It must also have pleased many young women
to be free from the control or interference of
their own mothers, although such freedom was
often truly established only with the birth of
their first child. 'I refuse to wear the blanket or
be *said* by anyone. I am a married woman ... ,'
declares Sissy O'Brien in *The Farm by Lough
Gur*.

SELECT BIBLIOGRAPHY

Ballard, Linda May. *Forgetting Frolic: Marriage Traditions in Ireland*. Belfast: The Institute of Irish Studies and The Folklore Society, 1998.

Bluett, Anthony. *Ireland in Love*. Cork and Dublin: Mercier Press, 1995.

Buchanan, R. H. 'Calendar Customs', *Ulster Folklife*, viii, 1963, ix, 1963.

Carbery, Mary. *The Farm by Lough Gur*. Cork and Dublin: Mercier Press, 1973.

Danaher, Kevin. *The Year in Ireland: Irish Calendar Customs*. Cork and Dublin: Mercier Press, 1972.

Danaher, Kevin. *In Ireland Long Ago*. Cork and Dublin: Mercier Press, 1964.

Hall, Mr and Mrs S. C. *Ireland, Its Scenery and Character*. London, 1841–3.

Hickey, Donal, *Stone Mad for Music: the Sliabh Luachra Story*. Dublin: Marino Books, 1999.

Keane, John B. *Sive* (revised text), in *Three Plays*. Cork and Dublin: Mercier Press, 1990.

Kelly, Éamon. *The Apprentice*. Dublin: Marino Books, 1995.

Kelly, Éamon. *Ireland's Master Storyteller: the Collected Stories of Éamon Kelly*. Dublin: Marino Books, 1998.

MacMahon, Bryan (trans.). *Peig: the Autobiography of Peig Sayers of the Great Blasket Island*. Dublin: The Talbot Press, 1974.

Mahon, Bríd. *Rich and Rare: the Story of Irish Dress*. Cork and Dublin: Mercier Press, 2000.

Murphy, Michael J. *At Slieve Gullion's Foot*. Dundalk, 1940.

Ní Shúilleabháin, Eilís. *Letters from the Great Blasket*. Cork and Dublin: Mercier Press, 1978.

O'Farrell, Padraic. *Superstitions of the Irish Country People*. Cork and Dublin: Mercier Press, 1978.

O'Farrell, Padraic. *Irish Proverbs and Sayings*. Cork and Dublin: Mercier Press, 1980.

Wilde, Lady. *Quaint Irish Customs and Superstitions*. Cork and Dublin: Mercier Press, 1988.